I MISSED MY OLD LIFE

CORRIE HARRIS AND DEBRA HARRIS

Archway Publishing books may be ordered through booksellers or by contacting:

Archway Publishing
1663 Liberty Drive
Bloomington, IN 47403
www.archwaypublishing.com
844-669-3957

ISBN: 978-1-6657-2570-5 (sc)
ISBN: 978-1-6657-2571-2 (hc)
ISBN: 978-1-6657-2569-9 (e)

Print information available on the last page.

Archway Publishing rev. date: 11/19/2022

Hi! This is Audie, I am eight years old, and I want you to see the pandemic through my eyes. My street was so beautiful and full of life. You could come outside and stand on the porch and say good morning loud. The neighbors would say good morning back those across the street would wave and smile, even those I did not know their names. The old people would be sitting on the porch reading the paper or drinking coffee. Others are working in their yards; the kids would be playing with each other or their pets. It looks like the sun shined so bright on our street; it has changed. The street is cold and bare, nobody is outside. The kids get off the bus and you do not see them again until the next school day. The neighbors are inside looking out the window. The sun does not really shine on the block anymore. I miss that joy and happiness you could feel just by coming out of the house and saying good morning to everyone and them back to me. This change I do not like when will the joy come back in our lives. We are showing progress with this pandemic, but it is not over. My sister said, we will one day just realize that it is gone, I sure hope so. Ladybug said, someday I will tell my grandchildren about this. Like granddad tells us stories about back in the day.

We are still at the window, what is it we are doing wrong? This is not ending. We are not working together as a country. All these separate groups do not want to follow directions. They do not have a solution to the problem, but they do not want to work with the groups. The groups are not keeping safe and just continuing to spread the pandemic. The lockdown was working to help keep the numbers down. Following the science, wash your hands, wear your mask and social distance. These steps are working. We waited for a medication, and they developed three vaccines. I thought everyone would be lined up for the shots. Then on the news there are people who do not want to get the shot. I am confused about adults and the way they do things. Now they want to get back to normal, how can we with only half the people protected. People are mean and violent doing all types of things in the stores, malls, and streets. We live sad the only place safe is behind the window

Audie "I cannot sleep, tossing and turning all kinds of thoughts running through my head. I need someone to talk too."

Audie "Asked Ladybug are you awake?"
Ladybug replied, "Yes!" What is the matter?
Audie replied, "I need someone to talk too."
Ladybug replied, "Okay. Why are you sitting outside the door?"

Audie replied, "I need to hear myself think or my thoughts will be replaying in my head. As a result, I am sad and afraid all the time. I do not like this feeling. Therefore, I am concerned about the family when we are not together and always questioning if you all are safe."

Ladybug replied, "What is wrong? Did you tell mom and dad how you feel?"

Audie replied, "This change I do not like how our lives have changed. It has made me sad there is no happiness anywhere. When at school, I cannot concentrate on daily activities. Meanwhile, I go in the zone and my mind is blank. It feels like I am sleep walking. The world is different, now we are going into two years and the pandemic is still here. There are vaccines available while numbers reveal half of the people do not want to take it. How are we working together?"

Audie "I do not like feeling this way. However, I do not want mom and dad to think I am a baby. Something is wrong, it not just me. The kids on the bus and at school all have that empty look on their faces too. I need answers. There are those people who do not want to stay inside, they try to make everything normal again regardless of people's health and that is not working."

The kids on the bus said they were not getting any shots because that is what their parents said. I do not want my friends to be sick. Another kid said, his grandfather said, the pandemic is not over the government is opening things to make money. Why did everyone's parents stop loving them? They are not trying to protect their children, friends, and family. People do not care about each other anymore. I wonder about my teachers believes. There are people doing crazy things to each other. They do not care about themselves or anyone else. I worry about you all, the pandemic, and the crazy people harming everyone. I wonder if I will bring something home, after being around these kids, with no shot. I worry about where I will sit on the bus, with whom I will play? I try to social distance, but it is hard.

The news people said, people want to take off their mask. Why? I do not want to take my mask off. This is a form of protection to fight the pandemic. Plus, the shot. I am afraid of getting sick. You know the hospital do not let your parents come in with you.

The mask, it can help keep you all safe from the pandemic. It is only a mask, but it is my only weapon to help. Furthermore, we are all worried because I know things in our house are different. Meanwhile, we are not happy, everyone come in wash their hands, take off all street clothes, and stay spaced apart in our rooms until dinner. In addition, there is no talking or watching television together anymore.

Ladybug replied, "You are right there are students at my school who do not have the shot. Also, when I am around them I feel uncomfortable, but when I come home I try to stay in my room to give the family spaced in cased I picked up germs. Things are trying to get better. More people are getting their shots. No one will know when the pandemic is truly over."

Mom and Dad enter the hallway. Hi! We overheard you talking, can we join you? They said, sure.

Dad went on: "every parent loves their children and try hard to do what is best for them. Your friends' parents believe what they are doing is right. People have medical problems and cannot take the shots. Then, there are those who just do not want to be told what to do. Yes, the government opened things back up because people need money to pay bills, their workplace cannot stay in business, closed, and people need their jobs. People need other people's help and cannot stay home alone or confined to stay inside. We are all afraid of becoming ill. This pandemic is coming under control, the science is working, the numbers are going down more people are getting the shots. We will beat this pandemic. I do not want you to be afraid in our home. Your mother and I want you to know love, happiness, and security in life."

Mother replied, "I am sorry that I did not stop and talk with you all on a regular basis. So, I can see how my children are adjusting to the changes in their lives. Your dad and I were talking the other night about how our home life has changed. We want our children to feel safe and comfortable in this house. We love you all and want you to know and feel loved. This is a new normal, but the fear is there, and we do not know how to get rid of it. However, in this house we will follow the science hand washing, social distance, and getting our shot. We do not have to be afraid of each other in this house. You should have peace and comfort in our home. We are your parents, and we work hard to keep this house and ourselves safe. This family is going to get back their joy."

Big brother came in the hall, "Ha"! Good thing I spent the night. Having a family meeting, without me."

Dad explained to big brother about Audie having problems sleeping and he was worried about the family getting sick.

Big brother replied, "I had the same worries too. Which include problems, sleeping at night. I guest we all have worries that will be with us. I decided to start a hobby to keep my mind occupied when I am home alone."

The family replied, "What is it?" Cooking.

Everyone replied, "Cooking!"

Big brother replied, "there is this guy on T.V. he has cooking classes and every night I cook a great meal. Big brother is getting to be quite the cook. Ladybug is becoming a music mixer. She sends me great music. For example, you should make Audie a variety of music that he could listen too; he would like that."

Dad replied, "we stop doing family things, but that is going to change family fun is back in this house."

Audie replied, "The people on the news argue about wearing a mask."

Dad replied, "we will wear our mask until we are comfortable without it. I do not want my family living in fear, nobody wants that. However, the pandemic is not gone, and all the people are not working together. We need to do our part to keep each other safe. I can not make the outside world normal, but I can make inside my home normal, putting back joy, peace, and security in my home. We all must work together as one in this house, to restore our children's security in how we manage their lives. I am sure every parent loves their children and believe that what they are doing is right for themselves. Also, is good for their kids. There are people not adjusting well to change, and they need medical help. Whenever anyone of you is having problems we will sit in this hallway and try to figure it out. Just say we need to meet in the hall, and we will be there."

Mother replied, "Well! Audie is fast to sleep, we all need to go to sleep."

Dad replied, "This pandemic has been a change for us. We need to stay a breast of our children's emotional adjustment to the conditions around them. Make a conversation about what they see and hear on the news. Helping them to understand and find out what they are thinking or feeling. Making things clear of what the schools, government, and society are going through. Any problems anyone has we will bring it to the hallway to find an understanding or answers."

This pandemic has side effects that we had no idea about or how to deal with them. People are not themselves anymore.

Printed in the United States
by Baker & Taylor Publisher Services